C000119289

Nail It In 90
90 days + accountability + celebration

Kim Johnson

Copyright © 2014 Kim Johnson
All rights reserved.

ISBN: 0692304894

To my sweet man, Mark,
without your love, your guidance, and your endless patience for
reading this book, I would not have made it happen.
I love you more than I could ever begin to express in mere words.

Table of contents

Welcome

I am so happy that you have made the choice to join Nail It In 90! Nothing is more satisfying than setting a goal and making it happen. Nail It In 90 has been designed to have you take this process and condense it into a systematic way of achieving your outcome.

After spending the last seventeen years in the self-development industry, traveling the world, and coaching thousands of people, I came to the realization that 90 days of focus is the best way to achieve what you want. It is not a quick fix. It is not always easy. It is ALWAYS amazingly satisfying after. I used this process to create this book, complete a workout program, and relocate our family from Rhode Island to South Carolina, all within the same 90 day time chunk. It has become my go to methodology BECAUSE IT WORKS. As I have worked to incorporate this with my private coaching clients, the success rates of accomplishments have jumped dramatically. I have even gone so far as to have clients texting me intentions and results daily. All for outstanding results.

Part of my motivation for this work is to be able to reach those who need it most, the people who could not spend enormous amounts of money on coaching and seminars. I wanted anyone to be able to buy this book on a random Friday evening, devour the content, get clear on their outcomes over the weekend, and start on Monday. Simple. Easy. Productive.

The plan for you; read through the questions, answer them all, then read one page per day from Day One through Day Ninety and take action daily as is shown.

What's Next?

Everything you need to be successful is within this book and your heart. If you take both and mix with immediate action, you will see and experience changes in yourself and your life. The power lies within you.

You can record your progress and notes directly into this workbook or into a separate journal or notebook as we go. It is a wonderful tool to look back upon when you are on day ninety and beyond. We also have log pages on our website that you can download to keep track of your progress.

On my Nail It In 90 website, you will find additional options for how you can engage with us.

There are downloadable programs, on-line live programs where there are weekly calls for you to participate in, as well as a private Facebook group where you will be able to post your results daily and get inspiration. I monitor the Facebook group, answer questions, give encouragement and share what I am working on for myself.

If you still feel that you need even more personalized connection, my team and I are available for private coaching. All of the information about the addition programs can be found by visiting our website at www.NailItIn90.com.

Now you know everything we have to offer! No up-selling. No secrets. No feeling left out. You can participate as you see fit.

So let's get started. Your adventure is about to begin!

The Purpose Of Our Lives Is To Be Happy.

- His Holiness, The Dalai Lama

What Can You Expect?

My husband often reminds me, "Missed expectations are the road to disappointment". It always sounds funny to me when he says it.
I am sure that is because I build up most things very large in my mind!
For us to consistently be on the same page, I want you to know what to expect; so here you go!

1. This is not a cake walk; it will require you to be here with me each and every day.

2. Rome wasn't built in a day, nor will your successes be built in a day.

3. You are about to become the tortoise, not the hare. In the end, a constant effort always wins.

4. I will provide you with mindset strategies and distinctions.

5. You will provide the daily actions that will build upon each other, no matter what your project may be.

6. Execution is the name of this game. The more we execute on beliefs with actions towards the goals, the greater the results.

7. Throughout the book, you will see this symbol. These are here to highlight particularly important pieces of information. Please pay close attention to these call outs.

8. Whatever you have chosen to work on for the next 90 days, make sure you are passionate about completing it! It must bring joy to your very being just thinking about achieving it. Your intention and excitement matter so much when it comes to actual results.

9. Frustration will happen. So what? Keep going no matter what!

10. Day 90 will come whether you give it your all or not. I suggest you give it all. You can't imagine the feeling of pride you will experience just by completing 90 straight days.

Why Are You Here?

Everyone shows up in this action group for different reasons, but the truth is that the reason you are here is irrelevant. The only thing that matters is that you are choosing to move beyond your current condition. Nothing else but that simple choice matters.

Decisions shape our lives. Every moment you are alive, you make decisions: the choice to shower, how to dress, how to eat, where you live, what movie to watch. Have you ever considered how many choices you make in a day? It's astounding. A major study on the matter by Jan Glascher, lead author of the study and a visiting associate at the California Institute of Technology in Pasadena has found that we make THOUSANDS of decisions in a single day. How does it work? How do we make those decisions? According to Glascher, our brain relies on two separate networks to do so, one that determines the overall value — the risk versus reward — of individual choices and another that guides how you ultimately behave. "Cognitive control and value-based decision-making tasks appear to depend on different brain regions within the prefrontal cortex," says Glascher.

While all of this is fascinating to me as a coach, it only matters if we are going to make the information useful and relevant to our outcomes. Just like many things in life, just because you know something doesn't mean you will use it!

 So when I ask you, "Why are you here?" it is only the beginning. The real power is in moving BEYOND that reason and moving into your newly designed life that you created by CHOICE.

What Are Your Intentions?

Everything begins with an idea, a thought, a sudden burst of reason. When you transform that into a real intention, that is when you can change your life. The challenge for most is getting the idea or thought to move to purpose. Going from the abstract is not always as easy as it sounds.

Over the last few years, people have been under the illusion that all you ever have to do is think about what you want and BOOM there it is! That may happen sometimes, however, the majority of the time you MUST take action as well. Intention coupled with well-defined actions makes things happen! The entire equation is understanding WHAT you intend to make happen, WHY you want it, what you will FEEL when you have it, and the PLAN to make it so.

 The first step in the process is to create the vision you want to make happen CRYSTAL CLEAR. This seems like it would be easy. However, many years of coaching individuals, companies and groups have proven that clarity escapes most.

Most people know what they don't want. They understand what is not working in their world. That is the hang up; if you continue to focus on what is not working, you will only serve to create more of what is not working!

Uncovering the challenges is great when used to define what you do want. Defining yourself by your daily challenges keeps you attached to what you don't want.

Ask yourself "What am I committed to and resolved to create in my life?" and see what your answer looks like afterwards. Use those specific words, not, "What is my dream?" or "What do I want?". You must get beyond wants and dreams and go straight to commitment and conviction.

What Are You Projecting To The World?

This can be very tricky to understand within your sphere of self-awareness. Being able to look at yourself and honestly measure your behavior takes bravery and courage mixed with a healthy dose of self-love. When you make the decision to put yourself under the microscope for 90 days and shift your life, you must be willing to identify your current state of mind and see your daily actions objectively.

 While you may think you have an understanding of what you are projecting, the truth is that you probably don't. The vast majority of human beings operate only from their own view of the world, unaware that it's just their particular view. If you find that you are often offended, sad, or angry, then the challenge you face is figuring out what you are projecting that is allowing these emotions to show up in your life OFTEN.

All emotions show up for all people. The key is recognizing when they are here with us too often to be productive! When you subject yourself to less than resourceful emotions regularly, you will project those back to the world. They may not be the exact same emotion, but you will be something that you would not like to experience from another person.

Change begins to be possible when you are clear about where you are. Once you can see with honest and accepting eyes where you are and what you are doing to yourself, you can begin to transform. The key is to be very accepting of what your actions are and how they are affecting others. Never mind being mad at yourself for your present state. It won't help you. Start by acknowledging where you are, what you are projecting and choose to love yourself enough to change it.

Do You Love To Tell Your Story?

Human beings are very natural storytellers. Some of us are better than others at this skill. Most of us are fantastic at telling our life saga! We rejoice at complaining about how dreadful the traffic is where we live. The weather seems to get constant attention! It's either too hot or too cold. Shall I even mention our parents? My goodness, that will get people going, comparing one childhood to another. Now don't get me wrong, there is absolutely nothing wrong with telling your story. Being emotionally invested in your story to the point where you can't move beyond the conditions it creates in your life is the real challenge though. For example, if you grew up in a house where your mother spent her time telling you just how poorly you did most things, you may still be running from that childhood. That reality may have you avoiding relationships, or maybe you have become a stressed out over-achiever who has to be constantly moving, doing and producing.

To move beyond the past, you MUST emotionally detach from the story. It's just a story. The emotion is not the driver anymore. It happened TO you. You are NOT the story. You are NOT the action of other people.

Just in case you need to hear this; you CANNOT suffer enough to change the past. You need to detach yourself emotionally from the old story, make a choice to create a new story and get busy; that is the only way to create a new story. I truly am not trying to make this sound oversimplified. It is the foundation that builds forgiveness and love. You must respect yourself enough that the NEW story is more important and relevant than the old story. Make no mistake that this will take work! We are very attached to our stories. Making the break from them is not the simplest of tasks. They keep showing up like a jilted lover, crying, whining and pleading to be told again. Your new effort is to stop telling that story, whatever it is. The conscious choice to tell the new story is very rewarding and fulfilling when you CHOOSE to make the shift happen.

Write Down The Old Story You Tell Now.

Take a deep breath of honesty and write down the old story you tell. Get it out of your head and heart. It will serve to allow you to see how it is affecting you every time you talk about it with emotion or make it your excuse.

Go write it down now.

What Is Your New Story?

You have the ability to write the story of your life. You can choose how you want it to read and who you want to be. When you come to this awareness, it's liberating.

Most people live in their current conditions, never fully exploring what their new story could look, sound and feel like. That is a life in complacency. That is a killer of creativity. The challenge is to bust out of the self-imposed cage and explore what your new story may be! We become so satiated by what is currently happening, that seeing other possibilities is difficult. The key is to let your filters fall by the wayside. Take a deep breath and ask yourself "What is the new story of my life?"

This is the story that you will be telling the world at parties, at the grocery store, at a restaurant. It is how you will answer when someone asks "So what do you do?" or "How did you end up here?"

The best way to re-write this story is to be clear on the last section first - "What must happen for you to thrive?" Once you know that, you can create your new story: the one you can't wait to tell. Explore what makes you smile. Understand what you want the focus of your life and intentions to be.

Write the new story around the new focus. If you are overcoming a tragedy, such as a divorce or death, make a conscious choice not to let this define you. You are much more than the loss. You are a soul coming through the darkness to find light to shine in. Events happen to you; they are not you. Stop living in a cage to which you hold the key. Decide what you want to be remembered for in this life.

Open the cage door. It's time to fly.

Write Your New Story Now!

Now it's time to write down your new story. Before you do this, take a walk, get a drink of water, and take a deep breath. Close your eyes and ask yourself "What is the new story of my life?" Capture every thought without filtering it. Just capture. If you find you are struggling, get up! Move around, put inspiring music on! YOU CAN do this!

Go write it down now.

Where Is Your Urgency?

Urgency can be a friend or foe. When you live in a state of urgency day to day, it is your foe. It will burn out your adrenal glands, make you short tempered, and cause you to act as if you don't know yourself at all.

However, when used with a light touch, it can be the spark to motivate. Just as you finish a wonderfully prepared soup with a pinch of salt, the flavor bursts into life. If you have a flash of divine clarity that you have been complacent in your mindset far too long, urgency can make your butt move!

However, you must know what is driving your urgency. We all have reasons why we want to make things happen. It is my experience that there is a deeper, more exact reason called urgency that resides in your gut. It's the voice that says "If not now, when?". It's the knowing that you turned 30, 50, 65 and you are still not where you wanted to be by this momentous occasion. It could simply be that you have just had enough of yourself. The excuses, the behavior, the lack of progress up until this moment. Whatever it is, it's your urgency.

When you understand how to use urgency to your benefit, you can call on it to shape the mission, stay on track and get things done.

   So the question is, "Where is your urgency?".

Write Down Your Urgency Now.

Capture your urgency with a feverish sense of wonderment. It is the fuel you need to make sure you follow through with your outcome. Use urgency as a friend who you keep close but don't let live with you!

What Must Happen For You To Thrive?

It is not a normal question to ask yourself!

"What must happen for me to thrive?" is not something they teach us to ask in school. In fact, I have gone the majority of my life NEVER having been asked that question. If I had, my life surely would have been different.

As I sit working on this book for you, that question is a driving force in my family currently. My husband and I asked that question, never really expecting the results we found. We are now moving from Rhode Island to South Carolina. We are changing the focus of our lives and creating a new reality. We are going out on a limb - HAPPILY!

What we learned; we were not living what we love. While parts and pieces were exactly perfect, more were not. Even though we have been consciously designing our lives for many years, THAT question made us realize we had not taken it to the extent we needed.

We became very clear what was missing, what we were longing for in our home: gardens where we grow our veggies, chickens where we get our eggs, slower, happier and balanced time, milder winters a must, ocean life is a must, picnics at the beach more often than just in the summer, must welcome and love dogs, must have a kick ass creative art scene, outside the box schools for our children, must have lovely, friendly people. All of this culminates in a place to fulfill the "unreasonable" request of THRIVING.

While our quest is well underway, we are discovering, exploring and learning
 more about ourselves than we could ever have expected all because we choose to be "unreasonable" and to ask a question that very few people even know to ask.
'WHAT HAS TO HAPPEN FOR ME TO THRIVE?"

If you don't ask, you will never know.

Write Down What Must Happen For You To

THRIVE?

Let your imagination loose here! Capture every thought, feeling, wish, dream, desire. Whatever you may call it, write it down now. When you finish, sit back and breath. It is the map you have been looking for, it may seem chaotic, confused, unrealistic; so what? It is what you, that oh so special you, desire. Once you have this down, the key is to look at it and begin to see how you can make it happen, piece by piece. There is no rush. You can make anything happen one step at a time. Get writing!

Is It All About What You Focus On?

Every day you get to decide what you want to focus on. The problems, the solutions, the fun, the sadness. You find what you are seeking!

We have all had 'that friend' who complains about EVERYTHING! It's too cold, too hot, not enough salt in the food, the drive is too far...whatever it may be, they see it from the perspective of the negative. On the opposite side, it is rare to see a person who is always upbeat. When we do, we usually ask 'Why are they so happy?"

Being able to drive your focus is a skill we are born with but quickly lose as we grow up. Babies seemingly dive right into life without hesitation, laughing and crying, getting what they want, when they want it. Toddlers have a laser focus on whatever they love. They will sit and play, learning all the while, uninterrupted by their surroundings. As we move into grade school, something happens. We start to live into what the adults in our lives project. For me, I spent most of that time with my mother while my father was working. My mother was very much a worrier when I was young. She would often voice her worries out loud, to no one specific. I, however, heard every single word. I became afraid of the most RANDOM things; killer bees, heights, unemployment...things most 8-year-old children should not be worrying about!

It took me many years to regain control over my focus. It is still a challenge for me when I get into situations of extreme stress. A constant state of awareness will help us drive our focus to what we want, not what we fear.

 Become aware of your focus. Decide what is worthy of your attention. Become the master of your field of awareness.

How Do You Train Your Focus?

Every day we go about our lives, vaguely aware of where our true focus lies. When I began making it a personal mission to expand my awareness, I too was in the dark about what was going on behind the scenes of my mind.

Awareness is like chasing a butterfly. It's here; it's there. When it lands, it's stunning. Often you are confused where it went.

The secret is to have your INTENTION drive your ATTENTION.

Consciously tell yourself for example, "I am cutting the vegetables" and concentrate on all the details of cutting the vegetables. The more moments you find during the day to train your focus, the better you will become.

Your challenge begins now.

Who Are You Sharing Your Plan With?

When you make the choice to share what you are doing with the people in your life you run the risk of their "contributions". Contributions or opinions, whatever you prefer to call them, can have an impact on you. Sometimes it's great. Sometimes not so much! For some reason, we as humans love to talk about what we are doing.

I am of the belief that sharing your intentions with others leads to many hard feelings. For example, you are excited about working on a new direction for your career that is out of the box for you. You have thought about every aspect of what you would like it to incorporate. The more you think about it, the more excited you become! You decide to share this with a group of friends over lunch. The responses; "What makes you think you can get all of this?" "Who do you think is going to give this to you?" "WOW, you're not asking for much (sarcasm)!" "In this economy?", blah, blah, blah. Before you know it, you feel as though someone sucked the air out of the room.

Can you remember this happening in your life? I know I can!

So now I take an entirely different approach. I don't share ideas and plans with anyone outside of a select few people in my life. The few that I do share with are those who I consider being in my inner circle, a 'pre-approved' group that lives in possibilities, as well as happiness.

Begin to create your inner circle. Decide from your friends who has what you are looking for in an actual support system. If you don't have anyone that meets your criteria, then don't talk about your outcomes until you are well underway, and you are not turning back. Being quiet takes getting used to for some. However, the results are worth every bit. Funny thing, though, once you start looking for that support system, you usually find it.

What Will Prevent You From Completing 90 Days?

It may sound like a downright dumb question. Why would I ask you what will stop you when I want you to get going and complete your 90 days?

Because you already know before we start if you will finish.
Now STOP. THINK ABOUT THAT FOR A MOMENT.
You already know whether you will succeed with your 90 days.

When we make decisions and choose to do something, we already know in our gut whether or not we will do it. We understand our level of commitment immediately. Some will argue that they wanted it, but just couldn't make it happen; that they did everything possible and tried their best. I will stand firm in my position that when you make a decision to do it, you will move mountains to see it through. You will seek help. You will work hard. You will research and make IT HAPPEN. IT IS CONVICTION. Without conviction, you will allow circumstances to get in your way and clutter your path. If you pause for a moment and think of the times in your life when you JUST KNEW you would make something happen, you will see the difference. That difference, that distinction, is everything. It is the gap between success and failure.

I am asking you, challenging you, to make the choice right here, right now. Will you do what it takes to make your outcome happen? Are you willing to look at what will stop you so you can strategize how it won't affect you when it does show up? These are the moments that define your true intent. Make a choice for yourself. Be honest right now. YOU KNOW.

Where Will The Setbacks Take You?

Setbacks will show up. As I stated earlier, if you are committed to making this outcome happen, you will find the way. However, some belief systems will help you immensely when the inevitable setbacks arrive.

1. MAKE THE CHOICE TO WIN even before you begin. Make it a conviction.
2. Have the understanding and belief that there are lessons in the setbacks. Regularly ask yourself "What can I learn from this?" and listen.
3. Adopt an attitude of happiness in general for your life. No matter what the conditions are, there is certainly someone in this world which is far less fortunate than you. Think about how many people can not even read these words. You can.
4. Allow the lessons in the setbacks to help you make the minor tweaks and adjustments in your course so you can reach your outcome no matter the time frame.
5. Understand this journey is only for 90 days, three months out of the nine hundred and sixty expected months of your life! These three months could COMPLETELY change the balance of your entire life.

Your internal belief system is your guide for these 90 days. I suggest you take a serious, honest "state of the union" look at yourself, make the necessary adjustments before you begin and throughout the entire 90 days.

Smile. There are tremendous gifts in all of this!

What Is On Your Annoying List?

We all have annoying things in our lives: the leaky faucet, the rug that never sits just right and trips us daily, a cabinet door that never closes, plants that need to be repotted, Christmas lights that are still up in March, a bunch of socks without their match.

These make up our proverbial annoying list; the running list we internalize of items that irritate us, yet which we put up with! Things that annoy you clutter your energy. They block progress and creativity. They hang you up every day, and you know it. Every year my husband and I go through our lives and make an annoying list to fix what gets in our way.

My nemesis is LEGO. My son had his Legos EVERYWHERE. It only takes stepping on a Lego in the carpet once to realize you never want to do it again. I put this annoyance on my list a few years ago. My husband had a genius way of solving this. A king size white sheet with ALL the legos in the middle. Simply unfold the sheet on the floor when you want to play and fold it back up when you are done with it. AMAZING. Annoyance is gone.

Most of the time the annoying items eat up time and energy, causing us to take away time from what we want to be doing. Worst of all, they send us down the road of aggravation, leaving us in a less than desirable mood for our day.

The solution is to make your annoying list immediately. Know what you need to fix in order to move on in your life. I promise you, once you make the list and work your way through the items, piece by piece, you will feel liberated! Even if it requires hiring people to help such as an organizer or a skilled technician for the things you can't fix, it is worth every penny.

Write Your Annoying List Now!

The beautiful, annoying list! Find out all the things in your world that you are annoyed by and can fix! Get very clear on all the little annoyances as well as the big ones.

Go write it down now.

Did You Love Recess As A Child?

Recess. The word either strikes fear or love instantly! For the most part, my breaks in grade school involved games that I was not great at playing: dodgeball, kickball, softball… Do you see a theme here?

I was not great at games involving coordination. When my recess included reading, I was in heaven. I loved nothing more than taking my books and sitting under the tree and reading. I could go anywhere and do anything in my books.

Why am I asking if you loved recess as a child? I want to know if you take breaks as an adult. I want you to remember what you LOVED about recess as a child so you can associate with that happiness of a break and make sure you are giving yourself that as an adult.

Most of us don't take a break. We spend our days and evenings doing and being what is expected of us, forgetting to have fun. Fun is the necessary ingredient in a balanced life and is NECESSARY for a successful 90-day outcome.

What kind of fun are you going to incorporate? I am not just speaking of the jubilant celebration you will have at the conclusion of our 90 days. I am referring to daily celebrations of wins you will have throughout the process. To truly be as alive as a child is active, you must remember how a child celebrates. Just like the reward of the recess, reward yourself daily, maybe even task to task, as you achieve little daily outcomes that add up to the main result.

Recess. What will your rewards be? What will your celebrations be?

Write Your Celebration Now!

Fun stuff! How will you celebrate your wins, reward yourself and when? Remember the idea of the reward of recess? This is where you figure out yours. A square of my favorite dark chocolate is my favorite. One simple small square if I have completed my workout. A glorious day at the beach is my weekly reward. It can be simple.

Go write it down now.

What are your Cross Training Skills?

We all possess talents that we rarely consider. These beautiful gems are such a part of who we are; we just don't see and appreciate them for the value they bring to us.

For example, I have creativity on steroids. As a child, I was often told in school "Just do the assignment as given", not allowing any room for my creativity to come through. Even in art class, I felt very restricted. At home, my mother was bewildered with my level of creativity. While she always did her best to support it, she often didn't know how to handle my request for supplies to create. As an adult, my creativity came out in my photography and home. It feels so natural to me to design a place to thrive for my family. However, when it came to my coaching practice, I never connected the two. Early in my coaching, I never recognized brainstorming with my clients as a creative skill. Then one day, a very dear long term client professed how much she appreciated my creativity with her challenges. She went on to explain how much she loved the varied ideas, solutions and pictures that I painted for her with my words. It stunned me.

How did I miss this for so long? What else had I been passing by?
In that very moment, I sat down and captured in my journal all the skills I had that I believed could be cross-trained.

Today, I am a habitual cross-trainer. I am constantly looking for skills that can translate well into uncharted territory. How does someone's skill as a baker make them better in business? How can someone's abilities with computers help them with art shows?

Capture all of your skills right now. Look at how they can be used in other areas of your life. Keep checking in with yourself to see how you can maximize your gifts!

Are You Ready To Be Brave?

In order to make it happen over the next 90 days, you will need a healthy dose of bravery. You must BELIEVE you can do this. You must BELIEVE you will do this. You must KNOW that the next level in your life is on the other side.

Bravery is a choice. To be brave, you choose brave. Ask yourself "How can I be brave right now?". By asking the appropriate question, you align yourself with understanding bravery is a conscious choice.

Being brave doesn't mean not being scared. It means that you act in spite of fear, knowing that you will be frightened, and that it is OK! Even if you have never undertaken anything like this before, you will play full out and make changes in your life for the better.

Questions will arise; feelings will show up. You will be tired. Time will fly by, and you will wonder if you will make it to the end with your goal in hand. All the mind chatter will happen. Just keep moving forward. Keep doing what you have planned to do. Have fun in the process!

Most of all, be brave enough to begin! Starting is the hardest part. The first week is tough, the second is even more difficult. Breaking your pattern of inactivity is challenging, but doable! You have already taken the first step by buying this book and reading it. Congratulations. Now it's time to be brave, plan your next 90 days and kick some ass.

It's Time To Begin.

I am assuming you have completed all of the previous exercises and are now prepared to begin. The next 90 days will make a shift in your life if you play full out with the conviction of completion as well as the excitement of a child.

You are making a huge stride just by beginning the journey. Each day, with each step and each moment of focus on your outcome, you are one step closer to the desired result.

Nothing happens without the steps to make it happen. If you use the metaphor of building a house, you will see what I mean. You would not start off with an empty piece of land, hire a decorator, then take all the items you will use to decorate your rooms to the empty lot! There is a sequence to follow, very specific sequence: design, foundation, framing, inspections, electric, plumbing, sheetrock, fixtures, and paint. There are so many steps; most people hire an expert to take them through the process. A general contractor knows what should happen when it should happen and how it should happen. When you follow the plans, even though there may be setbacks, you will end up with a beautiful place to live.

It is about YOU creating that beautiful place to live within yourself, as well as, outside of yourself.

Follow the plan. Stay focused on finishing. Do the steps daily. Most of all, SMILE while you are doing it.
It is your life.
Make it a masterpiece, one step at a time.

Write Out What You Are Creating in 90 Days

The Action Path!

1. Capture your outcome with clarity. Become CRYSTAL CLEAR. See all the details. Even the smallest of details will help compel you to make it happen. Make the picture of your outcome BIG and BRIGHT.

2. Understand fully WHY you want this outcome in your life. What will you gain by achieving it? What will you feel when you get it? How will it affect your life?

3. What is your URGENCY?

4. What are the action items you need to take to make your outcome happen? It will be an ongoing list. It is the living "verb" part of your intention. Make the first pass on the list. Do a brain dump of everything you can think of at this moment. Don't allow filters to come up telling you that it will never work. CAPTURE all the ideas you have to make this outcome a reality. Don't worry if you seem to have too few ideas. They will come as progress comes.

5. Now look at your list of actions items and decide the order of importance. What will you do 1st, 2nd, 3rd.., etc.?

6. Break out your action items into groups of the 1st 30 days, the 2nd 30 days, and the final 30 days. Again, don't worry if you seem to have everything in the first two groups. As you work through the plan and build on the action items you have completed, more will organically come to you. Typically you will be adding to the list weekly.

7. Look at the action items and begin to transfer from this master list to your actual calendar for DAILY items to accomplish. It is a critical part of the process. Most things stay on the average "To Do List" and never make it the calendar. If you don't assign it to be done, it won't! Visit our website www.nailitin90.com and download the 90 log blocks to help you keep track of days and actions.

8. Set time aside each week to review your progress and adjust your strategy. Read the Daily Pages in this manual for lessons and reminders of what to do.

9. If you are so inclined and consider yourself to be a very visual person, make a vision board of what you want. Simply put, this is a collage of pictures and words depicting your outcome as you desire it to be. I love to make mine HUGE! Roughly 24" x 30", I create my personal map and hang it where I can't miss it daily. IN YOUR SIGHT, IN YOUR MIND, IN YOUR REALITY!

10. The absolute magic to all of this; MOMENT to MOMENT AWARENESS. Know what you are doing, how you are acting, what is being projected. Step into your flow of energy and own it.

The Sample Action Path!

1. **Capture your outcome with clarity. Become CRYSTAL CLEAR. See all the details, even the smallest of details will help compel you to make it happen. Make the picture of your outcome BIG and BRIGHT.**

I am moving my family to a place that is ideal for the outdoor lifestyle. It has seasons but not the heavy New England weather! Since being active is so important to us, this place has everything we love: kayaking, beaches, fishing, boating, hiking, lots of parks, beautiful weather most of the time. The people are friendly, open and happy. Most important, the school Lucas attends is amazing and geared to handling an active, inquisitive boy.

2. **Understand fully WHY you want this outcome in your life. What will you gain by achieving it? What will you feel when you get it? How will it affect your life?**

I will create this because I have been living my life in proximity, staying where I was born, instead of choosing what was best for my family and me. Many life conditions had me believing that moving was not possible, however now I am wanting to live by possibilities. This new belief will give my family a fresh start with limitless opportunities to create new successes. Every member of my family will be able to experience a new version of themselves. That alone makes me euphoric since most of my life I believed what other people believed about me. To decide what to believe about myself is liberating! My creativity will soar, my business will explode, and my personal life will blossom since I will no longer be holding my husband back from his dreams as well.

3. What is your URGENCY?

My first "urgency" came from my mother passing away. She lived her entire life on the same street, and while that worked for her, it could never work for me. I realized from her death that I had been living small, staying inside my self-imposed box. While my son is entering kindergarten; what would be best for him? My husband has asked for the last five years to try something different. I have always been the brakes; WHY? I saw a quote from Buddha, "The problem is you believe you have time" and it has haunted me since that very moment. Time can create urgency when you realize that time is the most precious, significant and beautiful commodity we have. It can be wasted or cherished. My urgency is to love my time.

4. What are the action items you need to take to make your outcome happen? It will be an ongoing list; the living "verb" part of your intention. Make a first pass on the list. Do a brain dump of everything you can think of at this moment. Don't allow your filters to come up

telling you, "this will never work." CAPTURE all the ideas you have to make this outcome a reality. Don't worry if you seem to have too few ideas. They will come as progress comes.

- *#1 Research an area of the United States that fits our needs and desires. The happiest place we can find!*
- *#2 Find a school for Lucas*
- *#4 Find a rental property that will accept two dogs and one cat*
- *#3 Find a renter for our current home*
- *#6 Research movers and moving with a rental truck*
- *#7 Organize the calendar around when his school starts.*
- *#8 Look at what kind of opportunities there are for Madison.*
- *#5 Once we find our happy place, plan a week long visit and GO!*
- *#9 Clear out all the clutter and things we don't need*
- *#10 Give away as much as we can*
- *#12 Buy tubs instead of boxes since we may be moving again at the end of the year*
- *#13 Begin packing all the winter stuff*
- *#14 Pack the balance of the house*
  - *#11 Arrange the actual moving week; trip 1 with the things, fly back, trip 2 with the pets and kids*

5. Now look at your list of actions items and decide the order of importance. What will you do 1st, 2nd, 3rd.., etc.?

See the # above.

6. Break out your action items into groups of the 1st 30 days, the 2nd 30 days, and the final 30 days. Again, don't worry if you seem to have everything in the first two groups. As you work through the plan and build on the action items you have completed, more will organically come to you. Typically you will be adding to the list weekly.

1st 30 days:

- *#1 Research an area of the United States that fits our needs and desires. The happiest place we can find!*

- *#2 Find a school for Lucas*

- *#3 Find a renter for our current home*

- *#4 Find a rental property that will accept two dogs and one cat*

- *#5 Once we find our happy place, plan a week long visit and GO!*

2nd 30 days:

- *#6 Research movers and moving with a rental truck*

- *#7 Organize the calendar around when his school starts.*

- *#8 Look at what kind of opportunities there are for Madison*

- *#9 Clear out all the clutter and things we don't need*

- *#10 Give away as much as we can*

3rd 30 days:

- *#12 Buy tubs instead of boxes since we may be moving again at the end of the year*
- *#13 Begin packing all the winter stuff*
- *#14 Pack the balance of the house*

7. Look at the action items and begin to transfer from this master list to your actual calendar for DAILY items to accomplish. It is a critical part of the process. Most things stay on the average "To Do List" and never make it the calendar. If you don't assign it to be done, it won't! Visit our website - www.NailItIn90.com and download the 90 log blocks to help you keep track of days and actions! Here is a picture of the actual calendar I used for our move.

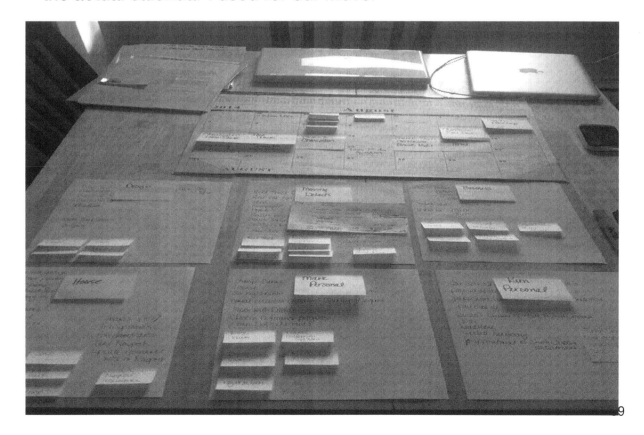

8. Set time aside each week to review your progress and adjust your strategy. Make sure you are reading the Daily Pages in this manual. They will give you continued lessons and reminders of what you need to be doing. Also, remember to visit our website to download your log block sheets to keep track of your progress.

9. If you are so inclined and consider yourself to be a very visual person, make a vision board of what you want. Simply put, this is a collage of pictures and words depicting your outcome as you desire it to be. I love to make mine HUGE! Roughly 24" x 30", I create my own map and hang it where I can't miss it daily. IN YOUR SIGHT, IN YOUR MIND, IN YOUR REALITY!

10. The absolute magic to all of this is MOMENT to MOMENT AWARENESS. Know what you are doing, how you are acting and what is being projected. Step into your flow of energy and own it.

Week One

Mantra for the Week - **Any Action Is Still Action!**

Quote

Don't judge each day by the harvest you reap but by the seeds that you plant. - Robert Louis Stevenson

Lesson

Today is the very first day our journey! Some of you may be excited. Some of you may be wondering what you have done to yourself. Either way, you are meant to be here. You are taking a leap of faith into the abyss of knowing yourself on a level very few individuals will ever reach. Most will not ever attempt a 90 day journey. So today be proud of yourself for even starting. Be proud of yourself for recognizing your needs and desires to be better than you were the day before. Life is meant to be fluid, ever changing. You my dear friend are about to change. Welcome to the new you.

Action

Day One is all about making the first move, whatever you are working on. Any action, no matter how small will make great changes when added onto previous action. Make sure your **Action Items** have been assigned for this week and get your butt moving. It's go time!
RECORD YOUR ACTION FOR THE DAY NOW.

Week One

Mantra for the Week - **Any Action Is Still Action!**

Quote

You are never too old to set another goal or to dream a new dream
- C.S. Lewis

Lesson

As you start this process, actually watch yourself with non-judgmental eyes. Freeing yourself from your opinions while you start will support you as you get going. We tend to be very critical of ourselves and our actions. This is not the time nor the place for that behavior.
Freedom from your own opinions will allow you to just do the work.

Action

Celebrate that you came back for a second day! Even though it's only Day Two, you have come so much farther than most.
RECORD YOUR ACTION FOR THE DAY NOW.

Week One

Mantra for the Week - **Any Action Is Still Action!**

Quote

With the new day comes new strength and new thoughts.
- Eleanor Roosevelt

Lesson

Your biggest asset right now is believing in yourself. If you can truly believe in yourself you can build your character. Your character will always set your standard for life. When you have high personal standards for how you conduct yourself, you have already made invaluable progress.

Set your standard high for completing these 90 days with grace and ease. Not only can it be done, it will be done.

Action - RECORD YOUR ACTION FOR THE DAY NOW.

Week One

Mantra for the Week - **Any Action Is Still Action!**

Quote

Don't watch the clock. Do what it does. KEEP GOING. - Sam Levenson

Lesson

No matter how you feel today, keep going. Action, no matter how small, will add up over time. To give you a simple visual on this, think about a dripping faucet. Drip, drip, drip...over the course of the entire day you have yourself a full bucket.
Your actions will add up over the course of this 90 days. Again, it doesn't matter how small they might seem. If they are on task and inline with your outcome, they just keep going.

Action - RECORD YOUR ACTION FOR THE DAY NOW.

Week One

Mantra for the Week - **Any Action Is Still Action!**

Day Five

Quote

Believe in yourself! Have faith in your abilities! Without a humble but reasonable confidence in your own powers, you cannot be successful or happy. - Norman Vincent Peale

Lesson

You have great privilege in this world if you are able to participate in this 90 days. As I have stated earlier, there are millions who could not even read these words, let alone be able to focus on more than staying alive for the day.

We sometimes forget that while our lives may be complicated, they are none the less a beautiful privilege.
Pause in appreciation for your your life, breath it all in and know that you are in the right place, at the right time.
Enjoy Day Five fully.

Action - RECORD YOUR ACTION FOR THE DAY NOW.

Week One

Mantra for the Week - **Any Action Is Still Action!**

Quote

Start where you are. Use what you have. Do what you can. - Arthur Ashe

Lesson

Look around and notice just how far you have already come in your life. If you think back over many years, you will find that the ebb and flow of successes and wins have worked to sculpt you just as water will sculpt stone. This can be a thing of beauty or can weaken structure. The decision which outcome will be visible resides within you and you alone. You decide how you show up regardless of the circumstances.

Action - RECORD YOUR ACTION FOR THE DAY NOW.

Week One

Mantra for the Week - **Any Action Is Still Action!**

Quote

The will to win, the desire to succeed, the urge to reach your full potential...these are the keys that will unlock the door to personal excellence.
- Confucius

Lesson

Congratulations. You have just completed your first week. Stop. Take a moment and let that sink in. You have controlled your focus for the last 7 days. You have taken action. You have rolled the dice and made 7 days of progress show up in your life.

My first 90 day stretch was working out. Everything on my body seemed so sore by day 7 that I had trouble even sitting down. On day 7 I was actually amazed that I had come this far. While 7 days didn't seem like a lot logically, to maintain the momentum 7 consecutive days seemed like I had climbed a mountain, mentally and physically. You are now well under way.

Action - RECORD YOUR ACTION FOR THE DAY NOW.

What have your "wins" been for the first week? Write them down. Celebrate how far you have come!
Go back to The Action Path; Read through the steps again, adding new items, working through the steps. Make sure you assign your action items for Week Two.

Week Two

Mantra for the Week - **Every Action Builds Upon Itself**

Quote

Infuse your life with action. - Bradley Whitford

Lesson

We make our view of our lives our reality. If you believe you will struggle, you will struggle. If you believe you can overcome anything, you will surely be much more determined while working to overcome obstacles. Stop waiting for your hero to help you make things happen. Be your own source of worldly inspiration. You have been infused with this skill from birth. USE IT. This is the first day of Week Two. Begin with a passion. Light your own fire this week.

Action - RECORD YOUR ACTION FOR THE DAY NOW.

Make sure you have recorded your action items from your list into your calendar for this week!!! SCHEDULE YOUR OUTCOMES.

Week Two

Mantra for the Week - **Every Action Builds Upon Itself**

Quote

Optimism is the faith that leads to achievement. Nothing can be done without hope and confidence.

Lesson

Manage your state. I tell myself this constantly. I tell my children. I never tell my husband...hehehe. This little phrase reminds me that it is so important to make sure we use our emotions as tools and do not let them take over, be our proverbial driver, unchecked.

Make certain that you are you using your emotions as fuel and not as a drainer. They can be either. If emotions came with a label, it would read 'Choose With Caution'.

Action - RECORD YOUR ACTION FOR THE DAY NOW.

Week Two

Mantra for the Week - **Every Action Builds Upon Itself**

Quote

Even if you fall on your face, you're still moving forward. - Victor Kiam

Lesson

What makes one action a win and another action a failure?
You. Your rules about winning and losing. Your definition of what things should and should not be. Not one other person can define your personal rules for you. You and you alone are in charge of your belief system.
Make certain that you understand what your rules of success are during this 90 days. They alone determine YOUR success and how high you will fly.

Action - RECORD YOUR ACTION FOR THE DAY NOW.

Week Two

Mantra for the Week - **Every Action Builds Upon Itself**

Day Eleven

Quote

Do you want to know who you are? Don't ask. ACT! Action will delineate and define you. - Thomas Jefferson

Lesson

Today's quote is one of my favorites. In order to be successful, you MUST take action towards your outcomes every single day. If you remember in the movie *Finding Nemo*, *Dory* sings a little mantra about 'just keep swimming'. This is the magic potion. JUST KEEP MOVING. Keep creating. Keep swimming. You are making progress, whether you can see it yet or not is irrelevant.

Action - RECORD YOUR ACTION FOR THE DAY NOW.

Week Two

Mantra for the Week - **Every Action Builds Upon Itself**

Quote

What you get by achieving your goals is not as important as what you become by achieving your goals. - Henry David Thoreau

Lesson

You are transforming yourself a little bit everyday. With this comes an array of possibilities. As you go from being the caterpillar to becoming the butterfly, your outcomes will be transforming themselves as well. Where you may have been seeing limitation on Day One, you may now see greater depth, more opportunities. Don't dismiss them. If you need or want to adjust your outcome, DO IT. The key is to understand what the reason is for the change. Acknowledge why, then decide. Everything changes. Embrace the process, including the changes in yourself.

Action - RECORD YOUR ACTION FOR THE DAY NOW.

Week Two

Mantra for the Week - **Every Action Builds Upon Itself**

Quote

I don't believe you have to be better than everybody else. I believe you have to be better than you ever thought you could be. - Ken Venturi

Lesson

I, like Ken Venturi from the above quote, believe we only compete with ourselves. I regularly ask myself if I am better than I was yesterday. It helps me to focus on me and not the external world that is constantly asking me to compare myself to others. I have no desire to compare myself, however, it happens from time to time. We are culturally driven to do so. It is not healthy though. Your only real competition is you. Don't worry about how you are doing compared to others on this path. JUST FOCUS ON YOU. I promise you will feel more peaceful when you let go and be you.

Action - RECORD YOUR ACTION FOR THE DAY NOW.

Week Two

Mantra for the Week - **Every Action Builds Upon Itself**

Quote

Change your life today. Don't gamble on the future, act now, without delay.
- Simone de Boeauvoir

Lesson

You have made it through the first two weeks. Smile. Take a deep breath in and realize your accomplishment. Fourteen straight days of action.

No matter what your outcome is, you have amassed fourteen action items in its corner. This is a now taking on substance. Just as interest compiles on a loan, you have now invested in yourself, most likely more than ever before.

Congratulations. You are no longer being led. You have become a leader.

Action - RECORD YOUR ACTION FOR THE DAY NOW.

What have your "wins" been for this past week? Write them down. Celebrate how far you have come!
Go back to The Action Path; Read through the steps again, adding new items, working through the steps. Make sure you assign your action items for Week Three.

 Week Three

Mantra for the Week - **I Am The Master Of My Days!**

Quote

Expect problems and eat them for breakfast. - Alfred A. Montapert

Lesson

From time to time, I will engage in random conversations with people about why they don't seem to be making progress in their lives. As I listen to the myriad of reasons or excuses, I think to myself, 'when will they tell me they just didn't make it a high enough priority'. The stinging truth is that we only do what we WANT to do. We barely do what we NEED to do.
All the reasons and excuses truly don't matter. What does matter is how you handle them. At all cost, avoid the excuses. Chew them up and spit them out.

As we enter into Week Three, take a good, hard look at yourself and see if you are working at a level that makes you proud. Make yourself a priority and just do what it takes to make your outcomes happen.

Action - RECORD YOUR ACTION FOR THE DAY NOW.

Make sure you have recorded your action items from your list onto your calendar for this week!!! SCHEDULE YOUR OUTCOMES.

Week Three

Mantra for the Week - **I Am The Master Of My Days!**

Quote

If you don't design your own life plan, chances are that you'll fall into someone else's plan. And guess what they have planned for you? Not much.
- Jim Rohn

Lesson

You cannot stop other people from living in drama. You can stop how you react to them and the attention you give to that drama. Every time you respond to what another person brings to you, make sure you do it without compromising yourself. Responding is a conscious, logical choice. Reacting is an unconscious, emotional self sabotage. As you begin to breakdown your old habits and rules, this will be a challenge. You may feel selfish for focusing on your needs. This is your reminder that while we all have responsibilities to our families, our children, our work, we must make sure we are taking care of ourselves as well or we are useless to everyone, including ourselves.
Just as the flight attendant reminds us every time we fly, put your own oxygen mask on first then help those around you.

Action - RECORD YOUR ACTION FOR THE DAY NOW.

Week Three

Mantra for the Week - **I Am The Master Of My Days!**

Quote

Your talent is God's gift to you. What you do with it is your gift back to God.
- Leo Buscaglia

Lesson

No matter what your spiritual beliefs are, you have a talent or multiple talents that you have been blessed with.   If you are not using them, they are dying. I personally do believe as the quote shows above, they are a gift. What you choose to do with them is your gift back. I feel unfulfilled when I am not using my gifts. If I am not coaching, I become mundane. If I am not being graphically creative, I feel like I am living in a grey world.

As we are walking this ninety day path, make certain you are using your gifts. They are there to enhance your journey of life. If you don't use them you will lose them. That would not make anyone happy, most of all you.

Action - RECORD YOUR ACTION FOR THE DAY NOW.

Week Three

Mantra for the Week - **I Am The Master Of My Days!**

Quote

If you are going through hell, keep going. - Winston Churchill

Lesson

Nothing about doing 90 days straight of action is easy. Having done this personally multiple times and coached my clients through the process endless times, this is a hard core reality.

Usually about this time in the process, your old patterns will try to come back. You may hear that wonderful little voice in your head say 'You can miss one day, Take a break. No one will ever know'.
YOU WILL KNOW. In order to break down the old patterns you MUST not let them take charge. You MUST stick to your intention. If you don't hold yourself to this higher standard, you can't expect anyone else to help you.

You must first show up for you. All the great stuff is found in this action.

Action - RECORD YOUR ACTION FOR THE DAY NOW.

Week Three

Mantra for the Week - **I Am The Master Of My Days!**

Quote

Things do not happen. Things are made to happen. - John F. Kennedy

Lesson

Every action you take makes something happen. It's really that simple. As you continue towards Day Twenty One, your actions are building. Think about that for a moment. They are YOUR actions, actions you have never done before with such commitment and intention. YOU are doing this. Not anyone else. You. Celebrate the fact you are becoming clearer and clearer on your direction with purpose in hand.

Completion of Week Three is just around the corner. Finish strong.

Action - RECORD YOUR ACTION FOR THE DAY NOW.

Week Three

Mantra for the Week - **I Am The Master Of My Days!**

Quote

Quality is not an act, it is a habit. - Aristotle

Lesson

Habits drive our lives more than we ever like to admit. It's hard to even begin to comprehend the hold they possess over us. To prove my point, let's do a little experiment.
Try to shower 'out-of-order'. Think about how you shower. I would bet money that you have the same habits for every shower you have ever taken over the majority of your adult life. Your 'wash' habits, where you hang your towel, how you dry your hair, even how you brush your teeth. ALL THE SAME PATTERN. Today, try to do it out of order. Try to do it differently. Watch and learn how this simple task fries your brain.

Now you know why you must be the master of your habits.

Action - RECORD YOUR ACTION FOR THE DAY NOW.

Week Three

Mantra for the Week - **I Am The Master Of My Days!**

Quote

Do not wait to strike till the iron is hot; but make it hot by striking.
- William Butler Yeats

Lesson

Review day. You have been working on your outcome for the past three weeks. I am sure there have been ups and downs. However, you are now able to tally twenty-one days of accomplishments. Write down what your wins have been. Even the smallest of wins count. Please don't discount anything. Capture your thoughts and emotions about the past twenty-one days. Truly see how much you have grown emotionally.

You have more in you than you will ever know. It is meant to be that way. Believe it and tap into that energy moving into Week Four. You are about to complete your first thirty days of consecutive action. Let's go.

Action - RECORD YOUR ACTION FOR THE DAY NOW.

Celebrate how far you have come! Do something for yourself that will make you smile, acknowledging your first twenty-one days!
Go back to The Action Path; Read through the steps again, adding new items, working through the steps.
Make sure you assign your action items for Week Four.

Week Four

Mantra for the Week - **Results Come From Congruent Behavior**

Quote

Be impeccable with your word. Speak with integrity. Say only what you mean.
- Don Miguel Ruiz

Lesson

You have begun the home stretch of the first thirty days. By this point, your typical patterns will have begun to be scrambled. Typical behavior is being challenged and replaced by desired behavior. You are understanding where you need to grow and where it comes more easily. You are still feeling a bit out of sorts however in a strangely excited way. This is all very expected. If you are having an entirely different experience thus far, guess what? IT'S FINE. You are exactly where you should be in your evolution of your personal life lessons.

I don't believe in 'right' and 'wrong' behavior. I believe in consequences. The effect of where you are right now is a direct result of acts or instances occurring earlier in your life. Managing your behaviors influences your consequences and thusly your final results.

Action - RECORD YOUR ACTION FOR THE DAY NOW.

Make sure you have recorded your action items from your list onto your calendar for this week!!! SCHEDULE YOUR OUTCOMES.

Week Four

Mantra for the Week - **Results Come From Congruent Behavior**

Quote

What you do today can improve all your tomorrows. - Ralph Marston

Lesson

Preparation mixed with action makes opportunity in my world. You are your own best hero. Without a doubt, you must take the action to make your life what you envision it to be. This takes initiative. It also takes character to manage yourself and live up to your commitment to yourself.

When all is said and done at the conclusion of our 90 days, the Quote for today is a outstanding reminder.

Action - RECORD YOUR ACTION FOR THE DAY NOW.

Week Four

Day Twenty-Four

Quote

Big shots are only little shots who keep shooting. - Christopher Morley

Lesson

One is never really defeated until one decides to be. If you have ever seen the classic movie, Cool Hand Luke with Paul Newman, you understand this completely. Paul Newman plays the role of Luke, a prisoner in a hard core prison camp, who flat out refuses to submit to the system. In the end, he died for his beliefs, but was never defeated.

Your attitude decides what the story of your life will be. Defeat is not something you can go purchase in the store and neither is success. Ironically, everyone's definition of both is different. If you are focused on the wins you are accomplishing daily, as well as what you can do differently next time the problems show up, then you are living with a healthy mental attitude.
Keep taking the shots. Keep focusing. Keep moving in life.

With this framework, you can defeat anything instead of it defeating you.

Action - RECORD YOUR ACTION FOR THE DAY NOW.

Week Four

Mantra for the Week - **Results Come From Congruent Behavior**

Quote

I would rather attempt to do something great and fail than to attempt to do nothing and succeed. - Robert H. Schuller

Lesson

As we approach Day Thirty, it is important to celebrate and it's important to recognize you have completed many smalls steps to create a shift in energy towards your outcome. With that shift comes the energy of having more opportunities 'falling' into your lap. It really is inevitable. They typically start arriving around this time and it can be challenging to remain on task. This is when you must refer to your original capture pages in your journal or notebook and check in with your outcome. See if any of the opportunities showing up enhance it, enlighten it, or reflect ideas that you have been contemplating.

Action - RECORD YOUR ACTION FOR THE DAY NOW.

Week Four

Mantra for the Week - **Results Come From Congruent Behavior**

Quote

One finds limits by pushing them. - Hebert Simon

Lesson

It is my personal belief that before opportunity shows up for you, displaying a magnificent package of success, it will test you to see if you really mean what you say. I have personally had this experience many times leaving me with a deep understanding of 'be careful what you say' for it will show up. Strength, confidence and personal power are typically built out of the ability to perceive where they were born; struggle. Just like it is hard to understand darkness without light, or calm without storm, success comes with failure.
Having this consciousness built into your personal guidance system will save you many, many hours of complaining to yourself.

Action - RECORD YOUR ACTION FOR THE DAY NOW.

Week Four

Mantra for the Week - **Results Come From Congruent Behavior**

Day Twenty-Seven

Quote

Perseverance is not a long race; it is many short races one after another.
- Walter Elliot

Lesson

Being able to coach yourself is a skill. Even though people may believe they know who you are and what you will or will not do, only you really know yourself. Our most intimate relationship is with ourselves. So the question is, why do we lie to ourselves? Not one other person is in your thoughts but you. The ability to tell yourself the many 'truths' that arrive each day is a gift. Not lying to yourself is really a necessary part of success. It's hard.

I had done this many times in my relationship with my Mother. I would lie to myself rather than handle my internal frustration with her health. We as humans love to soften our reality. Sometimes that is perfectly OK. Other times it prolongs the challenges by masking the real work needed to get us moving. Check in and make sure you are telling yourself the truth. Even though it's not easy, it will propel you forward.

Action - RECORD YOUR ACTION FOR THE DAY NOW.

Week Four

Mantra for the Week - **Results Come From Congruent Behavior**

Quote

Either you run the day or the day runs you. - Jim Rohn

Lesson

Plans. For the most part, everyone makes them. Few go as scheduled.
Why does this happen? The reasons are as varied as one's ideas.
I have a theory on this. We make plans to allow our need for certainty to be filled. As humans we love certainty. The trick here is to make sure you have a 'gut' intention to actually make the plans stick. While writing this book, a litany of disturbances show up during my scheduled writing time. I, however, made sure that EVERYONE in my home knew I was unavailable for anything outside my writing. This declaration gave me the clarity of my outcome, as well as my ability to disconnect from the needs of the house, while allowing others to step up and help me. I had an overwhelming conviction to my timeframe and the completion of this book.

Action - RECORD YOUR ACTION FOR THE DAY NOW.

What have your "wins" been for this past week? Write them down.
You are now TWO DAYS from reaching your first THIRTY DAYS!
Go back to The Action Path; Read through the steps again, adding new items, working through the steps.
Make sure you assign your action items for Week Five.

Week Five

Mantra for the Week - **Go For It Now. There Are No Guarantees Of Tomorrow.**

Quote

True happiness involves the full use of one's power and talents.
- John W. Gardner

Lesson

This quote makes me smile. The "full use of one's power and talents" sounds so divine to me. Living with abundance and using your talents enhances life's experience. It also brings up another idea of cross-training your skills. I love doing this.

If you have not made your list of skills as suggested earlier, what are you waiting for? This is your inventory, your collection of tools that will sculpt your next thirty days of rewiring your brain for unparalleled progress. Cross-training your brain is not only effective it's fun. It's a tool that many people don't know they possess. Make sure you are using all of your power and all of your talents. That is the universal calling card for "Hell yes, I am ready!".

Action - RECORD YOUR ACTION FOR THE DAY NOW.

Make sure you have recorded your action items from your list onto your calendar for this week!!! SCHEDULE YOUR OUTCOMES.

Week Five

Mantra for the Week - **Go For It Now. There Are No Guarantees Of Tomorrow.**

Quote

Day THIRTY!!!!!

Do not wait; the time will never be 'just right'. Start where you stand, and work with whatever tools you may have at your command, and better tools will be found as you go along. - George Herbert

Lesson

You have now completed your FIRST THIRTY DAYS!
What a major accomplishment! How are you feeling? What are you thinking?
What has changed?
What is going to happen in the next Thirty Days?

It's time to brainstorm, capture your next round of intentions.
Return to THE ACTION PATH.
Make sure you are revisiting your original capture, to add to, or expand on from this new version of yourself. Again, absolutely do not filter your thoughts. Just capture all of them.
Even though you did this exercise only 2 days ago for your Week Five Action Items, this is for your Next Thirty Days. Think bigger, think expansive.

Action - Smile! Thirty Days have come and gone. You made it!

Make sure you update your action items as necessary onto your calendar for this week.

Week Five

Mantra for the Week - **Go For It Now. There Are No Guarantees Of Tomorrow.**

Quote

Decide that you want it more than you are afraid of it. - Bill Cosby

Lesson

Moving into the second chunk, our Sixty Day group, it would be beneficial to understand these next Thirty Days will be different. If you have been playing full out, you are now in a flow of energy that has you making progress. Your old patterns have been radically interrupted. They are not likely showing up daily as before. You feel your confidence building around your end outcome. Your level of motivation is steady and committed.

If you are still having challenges, put your attention directly on your intention. Work to incorporate visualization into your daily routine as well as meditation. I personally do this daily with amazing results. Stay on top of your motivation. Even though it has become easier, you need to be acutely aware of what is going on in your mind as well as in your heart.

Action - RECORD YOUR ACTION FOR THE DAY NOW.

Week Five

Day Thirty-Two

Quote

Knowing is not enough; we must apply. Willing is not enough; we must do.
- Johann Wolfgang von Goethe

Lesson

Time can be distorted. Humans think that a month is a long time and a year goes quickly. The one fact about time that most of us are conscious of is that it keeps moving and evolving. Being aware of time helps you manage your outcomes and priorities. Obsessing over it can ruin your happiness. The point of making 'time' a priority is not to add stress but to build on your urgency to follow through and not delay.

I like to remember those who are no longer here with me to motivate me. Many of them had no idea their time would be cut so short. This awareness makes me cherish time, moment to moment. I am aware that time is a gift not everyone has the privilege of receiving.

Action - RECORD YOUR ACTION FOR THE DAY NOW.

Week Five

Mantra for the Week - **Go For It Now. There Are No Guarantees Of Tomorrow.**

Quote

You can't build a reputation on what you are going to do. - Henry Ford

Lesson

This quote from Henry Ford is here for my husband, Mark. He uses this theory all the time and I love what it projects. He will ask our children to specifically state their actions. He makes them think and speak, planning their actions. Action is the mother of building yourself, from the outside in. When I have a coaching client that is very stuck, we always move into action mode. Tony Robbins teaches that you should "act as if" and change will happen. Action makes you move your body, breath deeply, and get your blood moving.

Action does something else as well. It builds your character. You will never be the same person again, especially after Ninety days of action!

Action - RECORD YOUR ACTION FOR THE DAY NOW.

Week Five

Day Thirty-Four

Quote

I've found that luck is quite predictable. If you want more luck, take more chances. Be more active. Show up more often. - Brian Tracy

Lesson

Nail It In 90 is designed to stretch your limitations, to take you further than you have ever gone prior in your life. We are purposely engaging in this exercise for an unreasonable number of days to force you into change. This is not easy. You may be tired. You may be energized. It all depends on you and your interior landscape of thoughts, beliefs and emotions.

Make sure you are taking inventory of your everyday emotions. This simple action gives you a great way to see how your overall psychology is doing. If you find that you are spending time in less than resourceful states, make sure you change that immediately. Go for a walk. Meditate. Get some fresh air. Visit a park. Do whatever you need to do to brighten your mood.

Action - RECORD YOUR ACTION FOR THE DAY NOW.

Week Five

Mantra for the Week - **Go For It Now. There Are No Guarantees Of Tomorrow.**

Quote

Press forward. Do not stop, do not linger in your journey, but strive for the mark set before you. - George Whitefield

Lesson

Look for new connections that can help you on your journey. They have a way of showing up in disguise, so make sure you are on your 'A game'. The first step is to look inward and make sure you are in touch with your own gifts, using them to help others. When you reach out and help others with their outcomes, connecting on a genuine level, you will make heartfelt connections that will support your outcomes as well as theirs.

Reach out. Press on. Smile. Find your core connections.

Action - RECORD YOUR ACTION FOR THE DAY NOW.

What have your "wins" been for this past week? Write them down. Celebrate how far you have come!
Go back to The Action Path; Read through the steps again, adding new items, working through the steps. Make sure you assign your action items for Week Six.

Week Six

Mantra for the Week - **I Am Grateful For All The Things In My Life**

Day Thirty-Six

Quote

If you ask me what I came into this life to do, I will tell you: I came to live out loud. - Emile Zola

Lesson

Living out loud. This is such a necessary concept to greatness in your life. When you play small, no one wins. You certainly don't. No one in your life wins. Your outcomes suffer.

My definition of living out loud means you show up and abandon the belief in your fears. Fears may still be with you, chattering in your head, however, you are not listening with emotional attachment. You are unattached to the voice of fear.

Today, do something BOLD that you have been holding off doing. Make that telephone call. Write that blog. Be unreasonable.

Action - RECORD YOUR ACTION FOR THE DAY NOW.

Week Six

Mantra for the Week - **I Am Grateful For All The Things In My Life**

Quote

As we express our gratitude, we must never forget that the highest appreciation is not to utter words, but to live by them. - John F. Kennedy

Lesson

You have come so far. Take a moment and say thank you for this journey. Gratitude expressed is a wonderful release of positive energy. Every moment spent in gratitude attracts even more gratitude to you. When you live in that energy it is very hard to fail!

I would ask from this point forward that you make it a daily practice in your life to find expressions of gratitude. Saying thank you, no matter what your spiritual beliefs, brings a centeredness to your being. Make it a practice of choice.
There will be no regrets for this effort!

Action - RECORD YOUR ACTION FOR THE DAY NOW.

W_{eek} S_{ix}

Mantra for the Week - **I Am Grateful For All The Things In My Life**

Quote

Gratitude is the healthiest of all human emotions. The more you express gratitude for what you have, the more likely you have even more to express gratitude for. - Zig Ziglar

Lesson

When you express gratitude your world begins to evolve. The very moment you step into the place where your focus is on what you are grateful for, your entire energy shifts. People soften. Problems melt. The light begins to shine. The key to attaining this experience is finding gratitude for even the smallest of things, in the most unlikely moments. It's easy to be grateful for the big gifts in life. It is much more profound to be grateful for the fingers you use everyday! Look at your life and begin to unravel all of the things you see, feel, taste, hear and smell that you can express gratitude for right now. I find this has been most helpful in my toughest of times. As I direct my focus on something to be grateful for, somehow the problems just don't seem as daunting.

Action - RECORD YOUR ACTION FOR THE DAY NOW.

Week Six

Mantra for the Week - **I Am Grateful For All The Things In My Life**

Day Thirty-Nine

Quote

Feeling gratitude and not expressing it is like wrapping a present and not giving it. - William Arthur Ward

Lesson

I believe that giving someone the gift of positive emotional expression not only allows you to grow, it also gives the receiver the gift of appreciation. When you speak from your heart, telling someone how much they or their actions mean to you, you both receive immense waves of energy. This is not woo woo stuff. It is scientific in nature. Everything is energy. The energy of gratitude vibrates very high. The moment you engage this emotion, you match that vibration and the results are astounding. Practice this as much as you can. Begin by telling a waiter or waitress how much you appreciate their great service. Look them right in their eyes. Watch the magic unfold before you. This is one of my favorite things to do for people; share their greatness with them.

Action - RECORD YOUR ACTION FOR THE DAY NOW.

Week Six

Mantra for the Week - **I Am Grateful For All The Things In My Life**

Quote

It is through gratitude for the present moment that the spiritual dimension of life opens up. - Eckhart Tolle

Lesson

I do not feel we all need to share the same beliefs in life. The most wonderful thing about life is all the chaos and randomness that nature herself generates. Whether you are religious, spiritual, agnostic...it is all irrelevant. We all must choose who we want to be, what we want to believe and ultimately how we show up in our own lives. I personally walk on the spiritual side having been raised in a family that had a Catholic Grandmother, a Protestant Grandfather, a Baptist Mother and a Spirit Filled Father! I have landed on the side of love, compassion and gratitude. Nature is my temple. The sound of the ocean my sermon. Whatever you choose as your "grounding" please remember that expression of gratitude is the language of all hearts.

Action - RECORD YOUR ACTION FOR THE DAY NOW.

Week Six

Mantra for the Week - **I Am Grateful For All The Things In My Life**

Quote

I don't have to chase extraordinary moments to find happiness - it's right in front of me if I'm paying attention and practicing gratitude. - Brene Brown

Lesson

Searching my life for small moments to acknowledge has taught me so much. I am grateful for the daily "small wins" that add up to something momentous at the end of every 90 days. I am astounded at how my focus is the proverbial faucet for my gratitude, simply by choosing to put my attention on something magnifies its greatness. This also lets me recognize when I am off the intended mark. If I am feeling, lets say, less than inspired, I can always track my attention back to a poor center of focus and attention. On most days this is a moderately easy task for me now. It did, however, take many, many months of consistent readjusting to make it happen. So the challenge for you is to pay close attention to your focus and find things to be grateful for as much as you can. Even if it is the paper you are writing on, give it gratitude. Stick with it. I promise it gets easier.

Action - RECORD YOUR ACTION FOR THE DAY NOW.

Week Six

Mantra for the Week - **I Am Grateful For All The Things In My Life**

Quote

Joy is the simplest form of gratitude. - Kari Barth

Lesson

Choosing to be happy is not always easy. I am not going to lie to you, there are days that it seems impossible. This is simply the condition of being human. We have emotions. Not all of them are resourceful, however, they are all with us to guide us. When we work on cultivating joy in our lives, we actually make joy happen. Again, it's all a choice.

When I question whether or not attitude is something one can choose, no matter what the condition, I must remind myself of Holocaust survivors. I am in awe of the depth of love and compassion many of these souls possess. For me, just remembering the stories they have told about what they have endured, shifts my attitude. Joy shows up in my life when I call for it. Plain and simple.This is an emotion of choice.

Action - RECORD YOUR ACTION FOR THE DAY NOW.

What have your "wins" been for this past week? Write them down.
Celebrate how far you have come!
Go back to The Action Path; Read through the steps again, adding new items, working through the steps. Make sure you assign your action items for Week Seven.

Week Seven

Day Forty-Three

Quote

He who knows nothing is closer to the truth than he whose mind is filled with falsehoods and errors. - Thomas Jefferson

Lesson

Striving to clear ones mind of all the rules one has acquired over a lifetime will serve one well. While rules can help us, they can just as easily limit us. Most of the rules we have set in our lives are not rules we have personally chosen. They are rules we have be given by others as we were growing and developing. Take a moment, consider what rules you have that are now no longer serving to help you grow, but are actually stunting your growth. Much like a seed that cracks its shell, beautiful things will appear when you break from of your rules.

Action - RECORD YOUR ACTION FOR THE DAY NOW.

Week Seven

Mantra for the Week - **The More I Learn, The Less I Actually Know.**

Quote

Perplexity is the beginning of knowledge. - Khalil Gibran

Lesson

There will be moments of complete and total confusion in your life. Since we are just beyond half way into our journey, this can be a time of raw emotion when you are not quite where you want to be, and not quite where you started. Rules have been disturbed. You are performing at a level that is outside your comfort zone. You may not recognize yourself anymore. ALL IS WELL. This is part of the grand process of growth and abundance. When the moments of confusion arrive, CELEBRATE! This is actually a sign of release of your rules. YOU are now making headway, real headway. Keep moving with certainty you are headed in the right direction.

Action - RECORD YOUR ACTION FOR THE DAY NOW.

Week Seven

Mantra for the Week - **The More I Learn, The Less I Actually Know.**

Quote

Opinion is the medium between knowledge and ignorance. - Plato

Lesson

How often do you listen to the opinion of someone who is not qualified to provide you with solid advice? How often do these opinions send you off track, down a path you had no intention of heading down? Do these opinions set your emotions on fire, leaving you frustrated or empty?

If you find this is happening to you, please take a moment, hit the pause button in your life, and breath. Make certain that the people you are listening to are QUALIFIED to be giving you feedback that will shape your life! If they are not where you would like to be in life, ask yourself why you are listening to them. You may be surprised by the answer.

Action - RECORD YOUR ACTION FOR THE DAY NOW.

Week Seven

Mantra for the Week - **The More I Learn, The Less I Actually Know.**

Quote

All our knowledge has its origins in our perceptions. - Leonardo da Vinci

Lesson

How you see your world affects everything you do. It's that simple. If you can master this belief and live into it, your world will change. This works for better or worse. Once you have an understanding of what you truly "see" in the world, the world transforms. Ask yourself, "Am I waiting for success to arrive or have I been playing full out for the past 7 weeks?'. The answer matters. Waiting for success to find you is not the answer. Put in the effort and success will run right to you.

Action - RECORD YOUR ACTION FOR THE DAY NOW.

Week Seven

Mantra for the Week - **The More I Learn, The Less I Actually Know.**

Quote

The larger the island of knowledge, the longer the shoreline of wonder. - Ralph W. Sockman

Lesson

As human beings, we need to wonder. This is the space of greatness! Make time to wonder, to find yourself. In the process, capture ideas, thoughts, and feelings that will inevitably unveil themselves. I consider this time to be very precious to me.

Wonder is powerful. *The actual definition: 1. to think or speculate curiously 2. to be filled with admiration, amazement, or awe; marvel.*

To live in this place means you are not living by fixed beliefs! You have chosen to be in a place of POSSIBILITIES, the power place. Today make time to WONDER. It's WONDERful.

Action - RECORD YOUR ACTION FOR THE DAY NOW.

Week Seven

Mantra for the Week - **The More I Learn, The Less I Actually Know.**

Quote

The true method of knowledge is experiment. - William Blake

Lesson

Not everything you do will work. In the midst of what is not working, possibility arrives. When this situation arrives, welcome it with open arms! I have had wonderful ideas arise right out of what seemed like disasters. The idea for this book came out of a stressful situation. Instead of staying IN the situation and seeing what was not working, I asked "what could work" moving forward. Experiments began and WOOHOO, a plan with results in mind emerged. Trial and error is your good friend. Invite them over often. Never be afraid to fail! Failure just means you have executed. Success means you have executed MANY TIMES!

Action - RECORD YOUR ACTION FOR THE DAY NOW.

Week Seven

Mantra for the Week - **The More I Learn, The Less I Actually Know.**

Quote

Knowledge is power only if man knows what facts not to bother with.
- Robert Staughton Lynd

Lesson

Understanding what information and facts are relevant to you makes all the difference in your outcomes. Every race car driver has been taught that if he or she focuses on the wall, they will hit the wall! The wall is always there, sometimes within inches of where they are driving. That is a fact that they are aware of but don't focus on; they focus on the road. The slope, pavement, weather, speed, other cars, those are the conditions that grab their attention. Focus on the facts that matter to your success, the ones that will give you the biggest bang for your buck! The rest is just information.

Action - RECORD YOUR ACTION FOR THE DAY NOW.

What have your "wins" been for this past week? Write them down. Celebrate how far you have come!
Go back to The Action Path; Read through the steps again, adding new items, working through the steps. Make sure you assign your action items for Week Eight.

Week Eight

Mantra for the Week - **I Will First Lead Myself**

Quote

A genuine leader is not a searcher for consensus but a molder of consensus.
- Martin Luther King Jr.

Lesson

True leaders start with themselves. It is impossible to lead other people in a genuine, competent way, if you are unable to lead yourself. Leading yourself demonstrates in multiple ways that you are capable of self control and sound thought. One of my personal heros, Napoleon Hill, writes at length on this very topic. When you step into the leadership roll of leading yourself first, true vision is made visible.

Take a look at whatever you need to improve as your own leader.

Make certain in the process of the 90 days you are demonstrating your leadership skills with yourself first.

Action - RECORD YOUR ACTION FOR THE DAY NOW.

Week Eight

Mantra for the Week - **I Will First Lead Myself**

Quote

If your actions inspire others to dream more, learn more, do more and become more, you are a leader. - John Quincy Adams

Lesson

There are many things you just can not control no matter how hard you try. When you come to realize that the only real thing you have control over is yourself; your actions, your thoughts, your perception of life, you make a quantum jump in your personal growth. By living your life at this level you lead and inspire others effortlessly. Leading by example, void of words is what great leaders are made to do. While this is never an easy thing to do, it is the path true leaders walk. Remember Mother Teresa, Jesus Christ, Buddha...all chose to live by work before words.

Action - RECORD YOUR ACTION FOR THE DAY NOW.

Week Eight

Mantra for the Week - **I Will First Lead Myself**

Quote

A leader is best when people barely know he exists, when his work is done, his aim fulfilled, they will say "We did it ourselves". - Lao Tzu

Lesson

The silent acts of our lives have become almost extinct in the modern world. Tweeting, facebooking, instagram, along with countless other apps, have allowed us to inform everyone we know what we are doing, eating, seeing, and hearing in split seconds. This phenomenon has greatly increased the amount of information we share about ourselves. Having discretion is the key. Knowing what to share and how to share it will display your level of leadership skills instantly. Before you project any sort of an image about yourself by posting, make sure it is in line with who you desire to be a leader. Images are difficult to undo, social media posts are even harder.

Action - RECORD YOUR ACTION FOR THE DAY NOW.

Week Eight

Mantra for the Week - **I Will First Lead Myself**

Quote

Be a yardstick of quality. Some people aren't used to an environment where excellence is expected. - Steve Jobs

Lesson

When I think of excellence, I think of how that relates to my personal standards. I believe that in order to go through this life with any measure of success, one must choose to hold themselves to a defined set of personal standards. For me, I have them set very high. As a coach, it would be ignorant of me to ask my clients to raise their standards and not have mine set for excellence. The expectations I have are set by me and me alone. They are defined by what I have chosen to create in my personal world. Measure your personal standards for your life in all areas. Keep measuring and raising them. You will be surprised how this one small action can change your world all by itself.

Action - RECORD YOUR ACTION FOR THE DAY NOW.

Week Eight

Mantra for the Week - **I Will First Lead Myself**

Quote

Management is doing things right; leadership is doing the right things. - Peter Drucker

Lesson

I have found that most people like to think of themselves as leaders, however, very few are willing to do the work required to be a leader. This goes right back to leading themselves first, being the example others can follow. Putting this in action daily is imperative in your personal development. Push yourself. Instead of doing things "right", push yourself, make mistakes, reach for greatness by doing what it takes, making progress not perfection. This is the space where greatness shines.

Action - RECORD YOUR ACTION FOR THE DAY NOW.

Week Eight

Mantra for the Week - **I Will First Lead Myself**

Quote

A man who wants to lead the orchestra must turn his back on the crowd. - Max Lucado

Lesson

Possibly one of the hardest parts of being the example, the leader, is what you must leave behind. Sometimes they are habits, sometimes they are places, sometimes they are people. There will ALWAYS be something that you will leave behind. When you are growing, you are literally moving, so it is impossible to stay in the same place and grow. When I started on my personal growth journey over eighteen years ago, there were many things that had to change. This meant changing relationships with some of the people in my life. Not an easy task for the best of us. I had tough decisions, big outcomes, and higher standards I was working on. It was hard but necessary. As you evaluate your outcomes, make sure you are walking with the right crowd. As the age old saying goes, birds of a feather flock together. Know your flock.

Action - RECORD YOUR ACTION FOR THE DAY NOW.

Week Eight

Mantra for the Week - **I Will First Lead Myself**

Quote

A leader is a dealer in hope. - Napoleon Bonaparte

Lesson

Your mindset is a common theme during these 90 days. When you believe in what you are doing, truly believe, you are unstoppable. Think about dealing with a four year old child. They only know what they want, they are determined to get it, and they are willing to do what it takes to make it happen. They live in the NOW. As parents we know what that means. They are relentless. They rarely give up. They live in moment.
Are you as committed as a four year old to your outcome?

Action - RECORD YOUR ACTION FOR THE DAY NOW.

What have your "wins" been for this past week? Write them down. Celebrate how far you have come!
Go back to The Action Path; Read through the steps again, adding new items, working through the steps. Make sure you assign your action items for Week Nine.

Week Nine

Mantra for the Week - **I Never Give Up.**

Quote

Patience, persistence and perspiration make an unbeatable combination for success. - Napoleon Hill

Lesson

Thomas Edison. WOW. Thomas Edison tried and failed 10,000 times BEFORE he reached a solution that forever changed the entire world. Think about this for a moment. 10,000 times! This man had unparalleled resolve. He had a personal belief system that said every time he had a "failure" that was simply an elimination of what would not work. This level of commitment is rare. When we see it in someone, we love it. Steve Jobs. He had it. His vision, patience and commitment to the outcome changed our current world. How committed are you?

Action - RECORD YOUR ACTION FOR THE DAY NOW.

Week Nine

Mantra for the Week - **I Never Give Up.**

Quote

We could never learn to be brave and patient, if there were only joy in the world. - Helen Keller

Lesson

The above quote speaks volumes coming from Helen Keller. The world is full of dualities. We need them in order to appreciate and understand their opposites. Failure is a necessary part of success. For some reason we have been conditioned that failure is a bad thing. I say "Hell No!". Failure demonstrates that you are working on your progress. You are taking chances. You are making waves. Throughout these past nine weeks you may have had some failures. I am sure of it. I always do. They are just here for us to use like a compass. They are not meant to defeat us. The darkness is meant to show us how to appreciate the light.

Action - RECORD YOUR ACTION FOR THE DAY NOW.

Week Nine

Mantra for the Week - **I Never Give Up.**

Quote

He that can have patience can have what he will. - Benjamin Franklin

Lesson

Most people quit after three attempts. Three. Seriously, three.
Does that demonstrate patience? Leadership? Perseverance?

What is your personal average number for giving up? I am not talking about the times when you just know you must stop doing something because it is no longer right for you. I want you to determine a specific number of times you will attempt something before you give up. This is so important because this number will help you identify your commitment. If you will only make 5 attempts, you are probably not very committed to your outcome.

When it comes to your passion are willing to quit after a few attempts? Are you going to do whatever it takes to make your outcome happen? How committed are you? Are you committed to 10, 25, 50, or even 100 attempts? Challenge yourself. Know your number.

Action - RECORD YOUR ACTION FOR THE DAY NOW.

Week Nine

Mantra for the Week - **I Never Give Up.**

Quote

I'm patient. - Michael Jordan

Lesson

Today is day sixty!
You are two-thirds of the way there. The time to be patient is in full swing.
How do you manage your state during times when you need to be patient?
This can make or break your outcomes and most important of all, your soul.
When we live in constant anxiety it can eliminate any sense of patience. We
go to a place in the future, wondering and worrying if all will work out as
planned.
Patience lives in the NOW. It understands that the plans are in play, moving
along little by little, building each and every day.
Manage your state. Live in the Now. Stay patient. It will all be paying off very,
very soon.

Action - RECORD YOUR ACTION FOR THE DAY NOW.

Celebrate how far you have come! Move into the final phase with happiness
and love.
Go back to The Action Path; Read through the steps again, adding new
items, working through the steps. Make sure you assign your action items for
the final Thirty Days!

Week Nine

Mantra for the Week - **I Never Give Up.**

Quote

Patience and perseverance have a magical effect before which difficulties disappear and obstacles vanish. - John Quincy Adams

Lesson

You have now entered into the gap, the space when your old habits are no longer in control, your new habits are building their strength. These next thirty days will give you a completely new perspective on yourself.

This is the time for consistency. Do what you KNOW. Intend to finish strong. Fix your mind on managing your state at the highest level for the next thirty days.
Kick ass time is in full gear!

Action - RECORD YOUR ACTION FOR THE DAY NOW.

Week Nine

Mantra for the Week - **I Never Give Up.**

Quote

Genius is eternal patience. - Michelangelo

Lesson

When we study all the great masters that have come before us, they all speak of specific principles that we can adopt for ourselves.
In all of my studies, I believe that patience is the core of what all the masters not only understood, they lived it.

When you demonstrate patience you are ultimately exhibiting your understanding of what building GENIUS means.
In today's world of instant gratification, this is not a common trait! You must cultivate this in your habits and standards for yourself. Make it a point to maintain your patience. Prevent yourself from making the impulse buys. Curb your need for the quick fix.
Make Michelangelo a role model in your days and weeks ahead. Focus and patience invokes genius!

Action - RECORD YOUR ACTION FOR THE DAY NOW.

Week Nine

Mantra for the Week - **I Never Give Up.**

Quote

Adopt the pace of nature; her secret is patience. - Ralph Waldo Emerson

Lesson

Nature is the ultimate example to us. No matter what happens, it rebuilds itself. Fire, floods, volcanos, whatever may occur, Mother Nature rebuilds with love. There is never a hurry. She is alway meticulous with details, never rushing the process! Seeds have time to sprout, growing at their own pace. Looking over your plan, do you see yourself as the master Mother Nature is, nurturing your projects with love and patience?
Go back and infuse your coming days with a new understanding of patience and demonstrate it with yourself, your family and your project.

Action - RECORD YOUR ACTION FOR THE DAY NOW.

What have your "wins" been for the first week? Write them down.
Celebrate how far you have come!
Go back to The Action Path; Read through the steps again, adding new items, working through the steps. Make sure you assign your action items for Week Ten.

Week Ten

Mantra for the Week - **I Am Choosing To Live By Design**

Day Sixty-Four

Quote

Design is a funny word. Some people think design is how it looks. But of course, if you dig deeper, it's really how it works. - Steve Jobs

Lesson

Living by design. I am not speaking about what colors you paint your walls. I am talking about designing your ENITRE LIFE. When we started this journey, I asked you to figure out what you really, really wanted. Clarity is power. Recalibrating is a super power. Your ability to view the details and make adjustments makes you a creator. Doesn't that sound lovely? You are a CREATOR.
So the time has come to make sure no matter what you are working on during our time together, you pause and measure. Design and create your entire life.
Make is a masterpiece that is unique to you!

Action - RECORD YOUR ACTION FOR THE DAY NOW.

Week Ten

Mantra for the Week - **I Am Choosing To Live By Design**

Quote

Luck is the residue of design. - Branch Rickey

Lesson

I have often heard people make snide comments about successful people saying they were just lucky. I don't buy it. I believe that we create our own luck by living the principles we choose for ourselves. When you make sound choices, put them into action, all while managing your internal conversation, you make your own luck.

In the final few weeks of your 90 days, ensure your own luck by putting the necessary elements of luck into play. Make connections, reach out to people, live satiated in kindness, the core elements of luck!

Action - RECORD YOUR ACTION FOR THE DAY NOW.

Week Ten

Mantra for the Week - **I Am Choosing To Live By Design**

Quote

The details are not the details. They make the design. - Charles Eames

Lesson

When I work with my private clients one-on-one, we spend a fair amount of time on the details. My favorite metaphor for teaching details; pointillism. Pointillism is the technique of applying small, distinct dots of pure color in patterns to form an image. George Seurat and Paul Signac are the developers of this technique. This technique fascinates me every time I see it. When you are looking from across the room, you see the image clearly. When you get close up, you see each and every point. Every stroke the artist painstakingly placed on the canvas builds and build to reach the beautiful result. Miss one spot, you have a gap.

Does this make sense? Your actions are the points. Design with details!

Action - RECORD YOUR ACTION FOR THE DAY NOW.

Week Ten

Mantra for the Week - **I Am Choosing To Live By Design**

Day Sixty-Seven

Quote

Design is so simple, that's why it is so complicated. - Paul Rand

Lesson

There is an art to simplicity. However, making things simple is not always easy! Stripping elements away is a challenge for most people. We LOVE to make things more complicated than they need to be. Clutter and complication are the poison to great design.
I have made it a passion in my life to un-clutter my mind and my world. I have studied feng shui for its love of simplicity, form and intention. I have spent years cultivating my coaching style to incorporate all of what I believe are the key elements to success.
Look for the spaces to simplify. You will be surprised how freeing it really can be. Release the clutter and create simplicity!

Action - RECORD YOUR ACTION FOR THE DAY NOW.

Week Ten

Mantra for the Week - **I Am Choosing To Live By Design**

Quote

Recognizing the need is the primary condition for design. - Charles Eames

Lesson

In our world, there are 'needs' everywhere. Our own needs drive us to new experiences daily. Hunger often controls our day. As you begin to expand your awareness, even beyond where you thought you may be at this point, your time will be well spent reviewing your needs for the final push.
What are your primary needs right now in your life?
Are you designing the ideal conditions to fill your needs?
What has to happen for you to finish strong?
What do you need to do to increase your results?

Action - RECORD YOUR ACTION FOR THE DAY NOW.

Week Ten

Mantra for the Week - **I Am Choosing To Live By Design**

Day Sixty-Nine

Quote

I don't design clothes, I design dreams. - Ralph Lauren
Pause and think about the above quote. Do you understand what he is

Lesson

speaking about? The idea that it has nothing to do with the clothes and everything to do with the dreams of the person who buys the clothes?
This is an awareness that will serve you well when you make it part of your everyday life.
What is the underlying idea, design? When you are able to construct from this pivot point, the entire perspective of the design will shift.
Being the designer of dreams, especially your own, gives you a spark that will light the way for everyone in your life.

Action - RECORD YOUR ACTION FOR THE DAY NOW.

Week Ten

Mantra for the Week - **I Am Choosing To Live By Design**

Quote

Some men give up their designs when they have almost reached the goal. While other, on the contrary, obtain a victory by exerting, at the very last moment, more vigorous efforts than every before. - Herodotus

Lesson

The strong finish. I have been hammering this throughout the last 70 days. Why? Because it matters. Momentum is necessary to fight off the gravity of complacency. Continuing to design and refine throughout the journey gives you unbound effectiveness.

It will also serve you well to remember that while you are busy designing and creating, there are those who have already given up. How sad for them that they have not been able to see what you are seeing. Your efforts are a gift. Enjoy them.

Action - RECORD YOUR ACTION FOR THE DAY NOW.

What have your "wins" been for this week? Write them down.
Celebrate how far you have come!
Go back to The Action Path; Read through the steps again, adding new items, working through the steps. Make sure you assign your action items for Week Eleven.

Week Eleven

Mantra for the Week - **I Am Truly Stronger Than I Know**

Quote

We gain strength, and courage, and confidence by each experience in which we really stop and look fear in the face...we must do what we think we cannot. - Eleanor Roosevelt

Lesson

Reaching beyond your conditions in life takes courage. To go boldly into the uncharted territory of ones POSSIBLE self means you need to be brave. In todays culture, bravery and courage are not typical. Blending in, not being seen, that seems to have the most value for many. I ofter hear "I don't want to make waves", which just makes my soul ache. Making waves is what needs to be done!

If there are actions you have yet to take that you KNOW you should be taking, BE BRAVE. Plan to take those actions over the next two weeks. Finish strong and live in courage.

Action - RECORD YOUR ACTION FOR THE DAY NOW.

Week Eleven

Mantra for the Week - **I Am Truly Stronger Than I Know**

Quote

Do not pray for easy lives. Pray to be stronger men. - John F. Kennedy

Lesson

Remember when I spoke about duality, needing the dark to appreciate the light? This applies here as well, to move beyond the challenges of the final weeks. If you were a miner, you would be within inches of the gold right now. Your arms would be aching, Your throat would be dry with soil. Your eyes would be watering from the dust. Your pick may even be dull at this stage of the game. What is important now is not to give up! We are on day seventy-two and day ninety is right around the corner. The challenges will make you a force to be reckoned with.

Action - RECORD YOUR ACTION FOR THE DAY NOW.

Week Eleven

Mantra for the Week - **I Am Truly Stronger Than I Know**

Quote

Only one who devotes himself to a cause with his whole strength and soul can be a true master. For this reason mastery demands all of a person.
- Albert Einstein

Lesson

Mastery of your world. It's not for everyone! This should be a bumper sticker. Most people would like to believe that they have it in them to be the masters of their world. However, it takes far too much effort for the average person to attain.
You must be devoted to yourself and your cause. You must be willing to go the extra mile as well as the unpaved extra mile while in your bare feet!
Am I painting a picture you can envision? You have an opportunity to go beyond yourself. Do it running!

Action - RECORD YOUR ACTION FOR THE DAY NOW.

Week Eleven

Mantra for the Week - **I Am Truly Stronger Than I Know**

Quote

Strength does not come from physical capacity. It comes from indomitable will. - Mahatma Gandi

Lesson

Every action is ALWAYS preceded by a thought. Even if you are not aware of the thought, it is present. Your will, your spirit, can shape these thoughts in time of need and pressure. I always loved the phrase "when the going gets tough, the tough get going' since it says so much in nine words. We get it immediately.
Are you among the 'tough' when the dung hits the oscillating wind generator? Oh how I love phrases like that!

Action - RECORD YOUR ACTION FOR THE DAY NOW.

Week Eleven

Mantra for the Week - **I Am Truly Stronger Than I Know**

Quote

You have power over your mind - not outside events. Realize this, and you will find strength. - Marcus Aurelius

Lesson

Marcus Aurelius walked this planet April 26, 121 AD - March 17, 180 AD. He had it correct all those many, many, many years ago. We can only control our minds. Trying to control anything else is humorous.

Have you ever had a toddler that does not want to eat or potty train? If you have, you have learned special lessons about controlling others. I had this lesson with our son. I have NOTHING to say about what goes in or what comes out. I passed through all of the possible emotions during the process of his toddlerhood. In the end, I learned to control my emotions, not him.

The power of our minds is really just beginning to be understood. I, however, am certain of one thing, you are in charge of your own thoughts.

Action - RECORD YOUR ACTION FOR THE DAY NOW.

Week Eleven

Mantra for the Week - **I Am Truly Stronger Than I Know**

Quote

Mastering others is strength. Mastering yourself is true power. - Lao Tzu

Lesson

Mastering yourself is a life long pursuit. It will not happen overnight. It will not happen in a few years. As I have told you before, the more you learn, the less you know. When you equip yourself for a journey and not a day trip, you will be serving yourself at the highest level. Seventy-six days seems like a long time, however, it's really a moment in your life. This continues to be less about the outcome you chose to work on and more about the person you are becoming moment to moment.

Action - RECORD YOUR ACTION FOR THE DAY NOW.

Week Eleven

Mantra for the Week - **I Am Truly Stronger Than I Know**

Quote

Kites rise against the wind - not with it. - Winston Churchhill

Lesson

Are you flying high right now or are you being tossed about as the wind blows?

There are great lessons to be learned in the challenges that arise in our lives. Upon completing week eleven, take this time as a check in, a space to look at your true reactions to the events of your current circumstances.

Having an understanding of your typical responses to daily stimuli makes your life balanced.

Capture what is working, what is not working, and what you can do to make your flight more enjoyable.

Action - RECORD YOUR ACTION FOR THE DAY NOW.

What have your "wins" been for this week? Write them down.

Celebrate how far you have come!

Go back to The Action Path; Read through the steps again, adding new items, working through the steps. Make sure you assign your action items for Week Twelve.

Week Twelve

Day Seventy-Eight

Quote

Do not dwell in the past, do not dream of the future, concentrate the mind on the present moment. - Buddha

Lesson

The present moment is all we have. There is so much to learn about this one subject. I have been studying it for the past nine years and feel as though I have only scratched the surface. While I am writing an entirely different book devoted to this singular subject, for now I will give you a nugget of gold.
WHEN YOU MASTER YOUR NOW IN GRATITUDE, YOUR PEACE, LOVE, AND HAPPINESS LIVES IN A BOUNDLESS STATE.
Choosing to live in the moment with your intentions and outcomes aligned is how you change your life. Practice being present in the current moment. It will automatically shape all your tomorrows.

Action - RECORD YOUR ACTION FOR THE DAY NOW.

Week Twelve

Mantra for the Week - **By My Decisions I Paint The Portrait Of Who I AM**

Quote

A life spent making mistakes is not only more honorable, but more useful than a life spent doing nothing. - George Bernard Shaw

Lesson

In my opinion, there are not any mistakes. Everything you do brings you gifts. It is your life's work to see them and learn from them. When you truly learn something, it is then your inspired outcome to put it to work in your favor. Some of us take longer than others to comprehend this, repeating actions over and over, wondering why oh why do these things "happen" to us!

What happens is us. We create these conditions all by ourselves by our choices and actions. The best and most useful thing we can do for ourselves is be completely willing to "make mistakes" everyday and then appreciate all the gifts they bring us.

Action - RECORD YOUR ACTION FOR THE DAY NOW.

Week Twelve

Day Eighty

Quote

Accept no one's definition of your life; define yourself. - Harvey Fierstein

Lesson

Day eighty. By now you are even impressing yourself. Others, however, may be giving you reasons to doubt your accomplishments. You may hear comments like "Wow, that's great, but are you as far as you thought you would be?". This is what people do when they want to make themselves feel better.

Define yourself by your personal rules and vision. Never allow another person to define who you are, unless of course you would like this person to live your life for you.

Action - RECORD YOUR ACTION FOR THE DAY NOW.

Week Twelve

Day Eighty-One

Quote

Life is really simple but we insist on making it complicated. - Confucius

Lesson

Are you still living with complicated rules and beliefs that have been showing up on your journey? If you have, I highly encourage you to just STOP IT. Enough is enough. You have come all the way to day eighty-one. If you have rules holding you back and preventing you from finishing strong and proud, don't you owe it to yourself to STOP IT?
You know if you have them. You know in your heart what must go. There is not one more moment for any B.S.
STOP IT. Do you get my point?

Action - RECORD YOUR ACTION FOR THE DAY NOW.

Week Twelve

Mantra for the Week - **By My Decisions I Paint The Portrait Of Who I AM**

Day Eighty-Two

Quote

Our life always expresses the result of our dominant thoughts.
- Soren Kierkegaard

Lesson

You can not hide from the results. Our thoughts dictate our outside world. Plain and simple. Each and every decision will manifest itself into your physical, visible world.

What are you thinking about all day long as we finish our 90 days together? Stop repeating the same useless thoughts that drag you down like a ball and chain. Practice daily with new thoughts and new ideas to finish strong. This will make you ready to do it all again!

Action - RECORD YOUR ACTION FOR THE DAY NOW.

Week Twelve

Mantra for the Week - **By My Decisions I Paint The Portrait Of Who I AM**

Day Eighty-Three

Quote

Every man dies. Not every man really lives. - William Wallace

Lesson

Really living is the name of the game. Doing and being what YOU came here to do. I believe that each one of us has special gifts that are meant to be shared with the rest of us. When you keep these gifts to yourself or don't use them, you are not benefiting anyone, especially yourself.

Really living is sharing yourself fully and wholly. Don't die without authentically giving it your all.
On a side note, only you know if you are giving something your all. Make sure you are being honest with yourself. It is the path to true abundance.

Action - RECORD YOUR ACTION FOR THE DAY NOW.

Week Twelve

Mantra for the Week - **By My Decisions I Paint The Portrait Of Who I AM**

Quote

The privilege of a lifetime is being who you are. - Joseph Campbell

Lesson

Authenticity is a word I find very overused in our culture. It has become a way of making an excuse for bad behavior. "I was just be authentic to who I am" or "it's me being me" is what comes up to mask a lack of kindness and compassion.

True authenticity is living from a calling of the soul. I once had a client tell me she painted because she couldn't run from it anymore. It haunted her every thought. That is authenticity at its core. She IS a painter, and an extremely good one.

Be grateful for the you that you are! Live into that vision and enjoy every moment of it.

Action - RECORD YOUR ACTION FOR THE DAY NOW.

What have your "wins" been for this week? Write them down.
Celebrate how far you have come!
Go back to The Action Path; Read through the steps again, adding new items, working through the steps. Make sure you assign your action items for Week Thirteen.

Week Thirteen

Mantra for the Week - **I Choose To Share My Happiness With The World**

Quote

Too often we underestimate the power of a touch, a smile, a kind word, a listening ear, an honest compliment, or the smallest act of caring, all of which have the potential to turn a life around. - Leo Buscaglia

Lesson

Welcome to our final week. You have come so far!
I decided to end with happiness for a reason. It is the most important thing we can share with others. Think about it; so few have true happiness.
So I ask you, what are you projecting? I love this action.
We have worked so hard at this point to shift, design and create ourselves and our world. Now is the time to share with love and abundance. This doesn't need to be a grand process. Keep it simple and filled with love. Reach out to people. Smile. Connect. Not only will you be fulfilling your journey with tremendous momentum, you will also be assisting another in beginning their own journey. How marvelous is that?

Action - RECORD YOUR ACTION FOR THE DAY NOW.

Week Thirteen

Mantra for the Week - **I Choose To Share My Happiness With The World**

Day Eighty-Six

Quote

We shall never know all the good a simple smile can do. - Mother Teresa

Lesson

How wonderful to think about modeling the kindness of Mother Teresa. She was willing to love and express love in every moment of her days. This is not an easy action. At this stage of my own development, I can't do this moment to moment. I strive for this daily, however, it is not as easy as it may seem. Our emotions lead us if we don't lead them, sometime leaving us with reactionary states. This rarely leads to love!
Aim for love and kindness. Even if every moment is not successful, you will have filled your days with more inspired actions than you could ever imagine.

Action - RECORD YOUR ACTION FOR THE DAY NOW.

Week Thirteen

Mantra for the Week - **I Choose To Share My Happiness With The World**

Quote

For every minute you are angry you lose sixty seconds of happiness
- Ralph Waldo Emerson

Lesson

Truth be told, happiness has always been a choice. When you share your self-realized happiness with others you are giving them one of the greatest gifts souls can share with one another.
If you have been so wrapped up in your own world that you are forgetting to spread some joy - SMILE.
Go out and perform some random acts of kindness! What better way to finish strong than by sharing joy with others.

Action - RECORD YOUR ACTION FOR THE DAY NOW.

Week Thirteen

Mantra for the Week - **I Choose To Share My Happiness With The World**

Quote

Most folks are as happy as they make up their minds to be.
- Abraham Lincoln

Lesson

Choose to be kind. Kindness leads to unlimited happiness. When you resolve to being happy and kind, others will be attracted to your light, participating in your journey. You will attract all the people you need for your success with this strategy IF it is genuine. You can't fake this. People can tell if you have their best interest at heart.
Seek and find those who you can indeed use your help. Your entire being will rise from this experience.

Action - RECORD YOUR ACTION FOR THE DAY NOW.

Week Thirteen

Mantra for the Week - **I Choose To Share My Happiness With The World**

Quote

The Constitution only gives people the right to pursue happiness. You have to catch it yourself. - Benjamin Franklin

Lesson

Catching happiness is an inside job. You can't buy it, find it, or trade for it. Happiness is the result of decisions we make for ourselves about what we believe has to happen to be happy.

What does it take for you to feel happiness?

How do you know when you are happy?

What can you do to make sure you are projecting happiness?

These questions will help you define your version of happy.

Action - RECORD YOUR ACTION FOR THE DAY NOW.

Week Thirteen

Mantra for the Week - **I Choose To Share My Happiness With The World**

Day NINETY!!! COMPLETION DAY!

Quote

Happiness is not something ready made. It comes from your own actions. - His Holiness, The Dalai Lama
Day Ninety!

Lesson

Congratulations!!! I am so very grateful and proud of you.
You have reached your outcome. It may not be perfect, however, it is yours.
This is the time to celebrate! Do something to commemorate this most auspicious occasion!
Above all else, remember that it has never been about perfection, only progress.
Take time for yourself and capture your learnings. Please share them with me on our facebook page.

You are AMAZING.

Action - RECORD YOUR ACTION FOR THE DAY NOW.

Thank You.

You have spent the last 90 days with me on this journey and I truly appreciate your time and your trust.

No matter what you have accomplished, making the commitment and taking the journey is the heart of all the lessons. Sometimes we have success and sometimes we fail, however, the way we show up during the journey is what matters.

You have done what most will never even attempt. It was not easy. It was not quick. It did not involve instant gratification. You still did it.

My heart is full knowing you are well underway to great things.

Always find a way to enjoy the entire journey, moment to moment.

Huge big hugs!
Kim

www.NailItIn90.com

19330937R00074

Printed in Great Britain
by Amazon